Employment law for the business manager:

A study guide

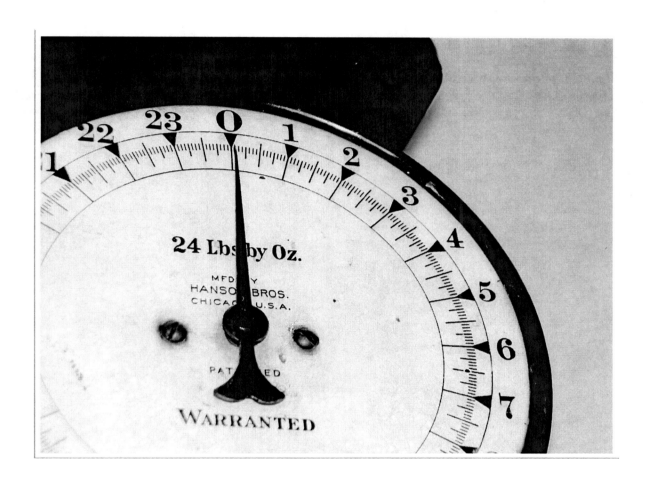

Griffin Toronjo Pivateau, J.D.

Third Edition (2016-08)

Cover image by John Mettraux

Table of contents

Introduction to employment law

Why study employment law?

Employment is one of the most important institutions in our lives

- It is our greatest - and perhaps only - capital asset

- Our economic and social system is based on the concept of employment

- It is where we form friendships and relationships

- Employment forms the basis for our identity

The study of employment law has additional benefits

- Employment law is a complicated mix of statutes, regulations, and case law

- Employment law is constantly changing

- The study of employment law teaches you how to think analytically

Employment law is about striking a balance

- The law tries to balance the interests of employers, employees, and society

- A decision may benefit one to the exclusion of the others

- Understanding how the balance is reached is vital for understanding employment law

Why NOT study employment law?

The sources of employment law

Introduction

Setting

- Understanding employment law requires understanding how the law works

- Every area of the law has sources

- There are three primary sources of employment law

- Employment law derives from constitutional law, common law, and statutory law

Objective

- In this lecture, we examine three important sources of employment law

Employment law is based in part on constitutional law

Constitutional law refers to the supreme law of the sovereign

- Constitutional law includes the fundamental law upon which the United States is based

- Constitutional law governs the creation and execution of laws by the government

- Constitutional law governs the scope of power and authority given to the government

- All government institutions, whether state or federal, must obey the United States constitution

- State constitutions are the supreme law of the state

Courts have the authority to decide whether laws passed by Congress are constitutional and therefore valid

- The United States Congress enacts laws pursuant to its powers under the Constitution

- The doctrine of judicial review gives courts the power to determine whether a law is constitutional

- The judicial system has the final say on interpreting the Constitution

Some constitutional provisions relate to employment

- The federal government's power to regulate employment is based on the commerce clause

- The privileges and immunities clause prevents states from discriminating against citizens of other states

- The first amendment to the bill of rights provides certain protections for the exercise of free speech

- The unreasonable search provision of the fourth amendment prevents some forms of search by employers

- The equal protection clause found in the fourteenth amendment may also affect employment

Employment law is based in part on the common law

What is the common law?

- The common law is also known as case law

- The common law results from judge-made decisions and interpretations

- These decisions form precedent

- The doctrine of *stare decisis* requires judges to follow precedent

Agency law provides the basis for the law of employment

- Agency law is fundamental to our legal system

- Agency is an agreement by one person to act for another at the other's direction and control

- There are always three entities involved in an agency relationship

Agents can make their principals liable to third parties

- Employees are (almost) always agents of their employer

- Agents can bind their principals for all acts within their authority

- Agents can bind their principals for negligent acts

- Employers often act only through their agents

- Not every agent of an employer, however, is an employee

Employment law is based in part on statutory law

What is statutory law?

- Statutory law is written law set down by a legislature

- A statute is an act of the legislature declaring, commanding or prohibiting something

- Statutory law reflects the will of the people speaking through their elected representatives

Statutes are a primary source of the law

- Federal statutes take precedence over state statutes, and state statutes are superior to the common law

- Statutes are subordinate to the Constitution

There are different sources of statutory law

- Federal statutes make up the U.S. Code

- Each state has its own set of statutes

- State statutes often supplement or mirror federal statutes

- Cities and counties enact municipal ordinances

- If state and federal statutes conflict, then the federal statute wins

Administrative regulations are similar to statutory law

- Statutory law is often enforced through the establishment of administrative rules

- Regulations have the effect of law as long as they lie within the limits set by the statutes

- Federal administrative regulations are gathered in the Code of Federal Regulations (CFR)

- In the employment arena, the Equal Employment Opportunity Commission (EEOC) enacts most regulations

Conclusion

- Employment law is based in part on constitutional law

- Employment law is based in part on the common law of agency

- Employment law is based in part on statutory law

Torts and employment law

Introduction

Setting

- Tort law is about the obligations that we owe to one another

- People rarely discuss the role of tort law in society

- Tort law defines the duties that we owe to others around us

- Tort law defines the remedies available when we fail to live live up to our duties

Objective

- In this lecture, we learn about the law of torts, how it regulates behavior, and about intentional torts

The law of torts governs the duties that we owe

People have certain interests that others have the obligation or duty to respect.

- These interests, and the duty of others to respect them, does not depend upon promises or agreements

- The violation of the duty to respect the interest is called a "tort"

- Tort law is the body of principles that defines these interests and duties

- Tort law defines the remedies available to the injured party when the duties have not been met

Tort law is different than contract law

- Contract law is primarily concerned with the ways in which private agreements will be enforced

- Contracts are entered into voluntarily and reflect the preferences of the parties to the contract

- Employment contracts are subject to public law limitations

Tort law protects important interests

The interest in bodily integrity.

- Examples of the violation of this interest are:

- Assault (causing imminent apprehension of an offensive touching)

- Battery (causing an offensive touching)

The interest in being free to move about.

- The violation of this interest is false imprisonment

The interest in one's reputation.

- The violation of this interest is **DEFAMATION**

- **LIBEL** (written defamation) or

- **SLANDER** (spoken defamation)

The interest in controlling access to one's home or place of business.

- The violation of this interest is **TRESPASS**

- The interest in controlling access to one's personal information

- The violation of this interest in **INVASION OF PRIVACY**

Tort law performs three roles

- Compensation of the victim

- Justice

- Regulation (Prevention of future costs)

The interests protected by tort law may sometimes be rightfully intruded upon

- We sometimes **CONSENT** to conduct that would otherwise be tortious

- Consent may be **EXPRESS** or **IMPLIED**

- The doctrine of **PRIVILEGE** acknowledges that some intrusions are justified by important social goals

- **IMMUNITY** reflects the view that for certain institutions, tort principles may be inappropriate

- Family immunity

- Charitable immunity

- Sovereign immunity

Torts often arise in the employment context

Many times employers are only concerned about statutory liability

- Managers and HR professionals often focus only on statutes

- Title VII of the 1964 Civil Rights Act

- The Fair Labor Standards Act

- The Family and Medical Leave Act

- The Americans with Disabilities Act

- The Age Discrimination in Employment Act

- Business people tend to forget common law liability

Tort law is not a source of employment law but it often acts in parallel with other types of law

- Tort law may provide advantages to the employee

- Tort law may provide a longer statute of limitation

- Both the employer and the employee can be liable for violation of tort law

Some torts commonly appear in the employment context

Defamation is a tort recognized across the U.S.

- There are three elements of a defamation claim

    - publication of

    - a defamatory statement, resulting in

    - damages

- Publication is a dissemination of information about an individual to third parties

- An employer who divulges private information to third parties has "published" that information

- Some jurisdictions recognize the concept of "self-publication"

- Publication may even be between employees and officers of the same company

- To be defamatory, the statement must be false

- The defendant may have a privilege

- An absolute privilege is usually limited to judicial proceedings

- The employer may assert lack of malice (a qualified privilege)

Wrongful interference with contractual relations

- A tort action may be filed against agents of an employer who interfere with the employment contract of an employee

- This tort is often asserted where an employer hires an employee who is subject to a noncompetete agreement

Intentional infliction of emotional distress

- Intentionally engaging in conduct so as to cause outrage

- This tort is often a supplemental claim in discrimination cases

- It is often filed in conjunction with sexual harassment claims

Conclusion

- Tort law is about the obligations we owe one another

- Tort law often acts in parallel with statutory law

- There are certain torts that often appear in the employment context

Ethics and the business manager

Introduction

Setting

- Managers face ethical challenges daily

- Managers have the potential to change, shape, redirect, and alter the course of other people's lives

- Managers make decisions that reward some with salaries, benefits, knowledge, and skills

- Managers will also engage in acts that harm people to various degrees

Objective

- In this lecture, we study the consequences that a business manager's ethical decisions will have for individuals, organizations, and society

What is ethics?

Ethics is the study of right and wrong behavior

- Ethics consist of moral principles and values applied to social behavior

- Ethical criteria can determine whether an action is fair, right or just

- In business, ethical decisions are the application of moral and ethical principles to the marketplace and workplace

There are different ethical reasoning approaches

- Ethical reasoning is the process by which an individual examines a situation according to his or her ethical standards

- Ethical reasoning aids in making morally ambiguous decisions

There are different ethical reasoning approaches

- Duty-based ethics

- Outcome-based ethics

- Corporate social responsibility

Duty-Based Ethics: Ethics based upon an underlying concept of duty regardless of the consequences

Religious ethical standards

- Duty based ethics can arise from religious belief

- Religious standards provide that when an act is prohibited by religious teachings, it is unethical and should not be undertaken

- The consequences of the act are immaterial to the ethical decision

Kantian ethics

- Immanuel Kant believed that people should be respected because they are qualitatively different from other physical objects

- Kant was not religious in the sense that we think of it

- Kant's categorical imperative states that individuals should evaluate their actions in light of what would happen if everyone acted the same way

The Principle of Rights

- Some hold to the principle that persons have rights (to life and liberty, for example)

- In deciding whether an action is ethical, one should consider what affect her actions would have on the fundamental rights of others

- A key factor in determining whether a business decision is ethical is how that decision affects the rights of others, including employees, customers, and society.

- One must determine which rights take priority

Outcome-Based Ethics: Ethics based upon the consequences of action taken or foresworn, without regard to any underlying concept of duty or morality

Outcome-based ethics are often known as utilitarianism

- Utilitarianism focuses on the consequences of an action, not the nature of it

- An action is morally correct where it produces the greatest amount of good for the greatest number of people

- A decision to act or not act should be directed to producing the greatest good for the greatest number of people.

Businesses often employ the utilitarian approach to decision making

- Applying utilitarianism requires:

- a determination of who will be affected;

- a cost-benefit analysis—an assessment of the negative and positive effects of alternatives on those affected;

- a choice among alternatives that will produce maximum societal utility (the greatest positive benefits for the greatest number of individuals).

Corporate social responsibility

The question of corporate social responsibility concerns the extent to which a corporation should act ethically and be accountable to society in that regard

- The Stakeholder Approach

    - Stakeholders include employees, customers, creditors, suppliers, and the community within which a business operates. It is sometimes said that duties to these groups should be weighed against the duty to a firm's owners.

- The Corporate Citizenship Approach

    - Corporations are sometimes urged to actively promote social goals.

    - Some companies publish annual corporate social responsibility—or sustainability, or citizenship—reports to highlight their activities.

Making ethical decisions

Areas to consider in making ethical decisions

- The law: Is the action you are considering legal?

- Business rules and procedures: Is the action you are considering consistent with company policies and procedures?

- Social values: Is your proposed action consistent with the "spirit" of the law, even if it is not specifically prohibited?

- Your conscience: How does your conscience regard your plan? Could your plan survive the glare of publicity?

- Promises to others: Will your action satisfy your commitments to others, inside and outside the firm?

- Heroes: How would your hero regard your action?

Applying ethical standards to employment decisions

Creating ethical standards for governing employment practices

- The business manager needs ethical standards for governing employment practices

- In creating the standard, the manager must decide whose interest it protects

- The manager must then analyze the problems arising out of enforcement of the standard

In any employment action, the manager should:

- Advance the organization's objective

- Recognize the issues created by executing morally ambiguous tasks

- Enhance the dignity of those harmed by the action

Advance the organization's objective

- Employment decisions should advance the central objective of the organization

- This standard requires managers to identify the objective that their actions are supposed to serve

- This standard provides a clear and consistent direction

Recognizing the issues created by executing morally ambiguous tasks

- Recognize the positive and negative consequences of an employment decision

- Recognize the moral sensibility of those required to carry out tasks

- Attend to the experience of those carrying out decisions

Enhance the dignity of those harmed by the action

- Ensure fundamental respect for employees by treating people with fair procedures

- Treat people in a consistent and equitable manner

- Preserve and restore the ability of the harmed individual to act effectively

Conclusion

- Ethics is the study of right and wrong behavior

- There are different approaches to ethical reasoning

- The business manager needs ethical standards for governing employment practices

Litigation of employment disputes

Introduction

Setting

- Disputes often arise between the employer and its employees

- Disputes between employer and employees are often settled in court

- Resolving disputes in court is called litigation

- It is important to understand the court system to manage employees

Objective

- In this lecture, we look at forms of dispute resolution used in employment law

Employment disputes may be resolved in state or federal court

The court system includes multiple levels of courts

- Trial courts decide the facts of each case

- Intermediate appeals courts focus on questions of law and not fact

- The decisions of a state's highest court on state law issues are final

The federal court system has three levels

- Every state has at least one U.S. District Court

- U.S. Courts of Appeal hear appeals from trial courts within their district

- The United States Supreme Court is the highest federal court

Similar procedural rules apply in state and federal court

- Every new lawsuit goes through certain stages

- Pleadings are the documents that set out each party's claims and defenses

- The plaintiff files a Complaint to start the lawsuit

- The defendant responds to the suit in an Answer

- The defendant admits or denies the allegations

- At trial, the jury will decide the facts

Appellate courts decide questions of law

How to distinguish a fact issue from a legal issue?

- A jury is required to decide what events actually occurred

- The appellate court is required to determine what rules to apply to the facts

- An appellate court must accept the facts as determined by the trial court

The appellate court follows its own rules of procedure

- Either party can ask the appellate court to review the case

- Each side argues its case to the court of appeals

- After having decided the case, the court will issue an opinion

- The losing party may ask the Supreme Court to review the case, but it is not obligated to do so

How to read a case

- Legal cases are identified by a "legal citation" (or a "cite") as in the sample below:

- Rent-A-Center, West v. Jackson, 130 S.Ct. 2772 (U.S. 2010)

- Every case contains the name of the judge who authored the opinion

- Every case contains a description of the facts and a statement of the applicable law

- Every case will draw a conclusion based on application of the law to the facts

The litigation of employment discrimination litigation differs from normal lawsuits

The law requires that a discrimination plaintiff go through an administrative procedure before filing a lawsuit

- An employment plaintiff must file a charge of discrimination with an appropriate agency before filing suit

- The Equal Employment Opportunity Commission is the federal agency that administers many federal employment statutes

- The EEOC oversees the enforcement of the following federal employment statutes

  - Title VII of the Civil Rights Act

  - The Americans with Disabilities Act

  - The Age Discrimination in Employment Act

- An employee with a cause of action under these statutes must file a charge with the EEOC before filing suit

The employee must meet the statute of limitations

- An employment plaintiff has 180 days to file a charge with the EEOC

- States have their own statutes protecting against discrimination in employment

- Most states have an agency that acts in the same manner as the EEOC

A state agency is called a fair employment practices agency (FEPA)

- An employee may file his claim (called a **charge**) with either the state FEPA or the EEOC

- The charge must include specific information

- Each agency has a prescribed charge-handling process

- The agency will usually immediately refer the case to mediation

- The agency then investigates the claim

The agency may do one of two things

- The agency may litigate the suit in federal court

- The agency may issue a notice of right to sue

- The employee has 90 days to file a lawsuit following the receipt of a right to sue letter

Conclusion

- Employment disputes may be resolved in state or federal court

- Appellate courts decide questions of law

- The litigation of employment discrimination litigation differs from normal lawsuits

Alternate means of dispute resolution

Introduction

Setting

- Increasingly, disputes are decided outside of the court system

- There are different forms of alternate dispute resolution

- Alternate dispute resolution is growing more important in employment litigation

- Recent Supreme Court decisions indicate that most employment disputes will be consigned to private processes

Objective

- In this lecture, we examine alternate forms of employment dispute resolution

Increasingly, disputes are decided outside of the court system

Alternate dispute resolution entered the employment arena through collective bargaining

- Until the 1970s, employment disputes were generally resolved in court

- Arbitration and mediation were often parts of collective bargaining agreements

- In the 1990s, more and more disputes were shifted into private processes

- Courts are willing to apply contract principles

- Case discussion: Rent-A-Center, West v. Jackson, *130 S.Ct. 2772 (2010)*

There are different forms of alternate dispute resolution

- Mediation is an informal nonbinding procedure

- Arbitration, a formal procedure, binds both parties to the result

- The parties may agree to a summary trial

- Judges may hold a judicial settlement conference

Arbitration is a formal means of alternate dispute resolution

Arbitration has been used more often in recent years

- Arbitration was once used primarily in collective bargaining situations

- The enforceability of the arbitration agreement is often litigated

- In this lecture, employment agreements often include an arbitration clause

- The scope of authority given to the arbitrator is often an issue

Arbitration is governed by statutes

- The Federal Arbitration Act governs most arbitrations

- Each state generally has an applicable arbitration act

Arbitration resembles a court case

- The arbitration proceeding is adversarial

- At an arbitration, the parties present evidence and witnesses

- The rules of evidence don't usually apply

Parties end up in arbitration in different ways

- The contract at issue may contain an agreement to arbitrate

- The parties may agree to arbitration at the time of dispute

- A court may order the parties to arbitration

Arbitration is generally a binding procedure

- The arbitration is conducted in front of a neutral third party or parties

- There is generally no appeal of an arbitration award

- Case discussion: Hall Street Associates, LLC v. Mattel, Inc., *128 S.Ct. 1396 (2008)*

Mediation uses a neutral third party to resolve disputes in an informal procedure

Mediation is designed to facilitate an early resolution of the dispute

- Generally all disputes are now subject to mediation

- The agreement at dispute may provide for mediation

- Courts will always order a dispute to mediation before trial

Mediation contains several advantages

- Mediation is a private, confidential, and inexpensive process

- In a mediation, the parties control their fate

- A mediation agreement may be enforced in a court

Mediation has disadvantages

- Mediation relies on each party having a good faith desire to settle the case

- Mediation does not provide an independent means for the discovery of evidence

- Enforcement of a mediation agreement requires court intervention

- Private resolution of disputes prevents the growth of the common law

Conclusion

- Employment disputes are increasingly resolved in private processes

- Arbitration is a formal means of alternate dispute resolution

- Mediation uses a neutral third party to resolve disputes in an informal procedure

Defining the employment relationship

Introduction

Setting

- The employment relationship has experienced numerous changes

- The employment relationship has become subject to greater government regulation

- The struggle between freedom of contract and regulation of employment produces conflict

- The question of employee status makes the regulation of employment more difficult

Objective

- In this lecture, we examine the evolving nature of the employment relationship

An employer can make employment decisions that are not based on wrongful grounds

The institution of employment is a fairly recent innovation

- Historically, laborers and owners had a relationship beyond mere employment

- These historic rules evolved into the master-servant relationship

- Under the common law, the master had a duty to give legal orders and to treat his servant well

- The servant had a duty to obey all legal orders

- The master servant relationship led to the concept of *respondeat superior*

Employment at will is presumed

The foundational principle of United States employment law is the presumption that employment is at will

- Either party is free to terminate the employment relationship without notice or cause

- Employment at will is rooted in the notion of freedom of contract

- Employment at will is the default rule in virtually every state

- In the United States, only Montana has a "for cause" standard

Case discussion: Payne v. The Western & Atlantic Railroad Co., *81 Tenn. 507 (1884)*

The employer's ability to terminate the employment relationship is still limited by statute

- An employer cannot violate antidiscrimination laws

- An employer cannot terminate an employee in retaliation for exercising statutory rights

- An employer's ability to terminate may be limited by tort law or by public policy

The United States stands virtually alone in its support for the at will employment rule

- In most other countries, statutes protect employees from "unfair dismissal"

- Often, countries have special courts that address these types of claims

- Some would argue that in actual use, the US system does not differ that much from the rest of the world

Agreements for a definite term would limit termination of an employment relationship

The at-will employment rule contemplates that the parties may negotiate over the term of their relationship

- Contract principles apply to this agreement

- Contract principles require offer, acceptance, and consideration

- The contract does not require identical consideration from both parties

If the parties specify a term of employment, the agreement will rebut the at-will employment presumption

- This is true even if the parties did not expressly state that "cause" is required for termination

- The contract must call for a definite term or the at will presumption applies

- A contract calling for a specified "annual salary" does not constitute a specified term

Employer promises may be enforceable because of promissory estoppel

Courts like the idea of promissory estoppel

- Promissory estoppel is similar to an implied contract

- Promissory estoppel requires a showing of "detrimental reliance"

- Promissory estoppel requires that the employer made a promise that it knew would be relied upon

- The promise must have led the plaintiff to act

Case discussion: Grouse v. Group Health Plan, Inc., 306 N.W.2d 114 (Minn. 1981)

Conclusion

- An employer can make employment decisions that are not based on wrongful grounds

- The law presumes that employees are hired as at will employees

- In recent years the at will doctrine has eroded

Worker classification tests

Introduction

Setting

- Most labor and employment laws apply only to employees

- The structure of the American workplace depends on the ability to distinguish between employees and independent contractors

- The agreement between the worker and the employer is of little help

- Courts use a variety of tests to determine employee status

Objective

- In this lecture, we examine the different tests used to determine employee status

The question of employee status is critical to understanding regulation

Proper employee classification is important

- Employment regulation applies to employees

- Numerous federal statutes apply only to employees

- The National Labor Relations Act

- The Fair Labor Standards Act

- The Employee Retirement Income Security Act

- The Internal Revenue Code

- The Family and Medical Leave Act

- Social Security Act

Any party seeking relief under these acts must be able to prove employee status

- Those classified as independent contractors fall outside the scope of most state and federal employment statutes

- Statutory regulations are of little use in determining employee status

- Under Title VII, the term employee means an individual employed by an employer

- The National Labor Relations Act defines employee as an individual who is not an independent contractor

Contract terms are of little use in determining employee status in determining employee status

- It usually does not matter what the parties call themselves

- Case discussion: Vizcaino v. Microsoft, 97 F.3d 1187 (9th Cir. 1996)

Why do employers misclassify?

Worker misclassification occurs because numerous financial incentives weigh on the side of independent contractor status

- An employer who uses independent contractors rather than employees:

  - can avoid union representation

  - not responsible for wages in excess of minimum wage

  - may avoid regulations

  - may avoid payment of fees and expenses

  - costs of withholding

- Some have estimated that employers can realize savings of up to 30 percent by avoiding:

  - payroll taxes,

  - unemployment insurance,

  - workers' compensation

  - disability insurance,

- pensions,

  - sick days,

  - health insurance, and

  - vacation time

- Most workers would prefer to be classified as employees

There are severe consequences to employee misclassification

- State and federal agencies consider employee misclassification to be a significant problem

- In recent years, there have been numerous initiatives aimed at employee misclassification

- Many states have passed laws aimed at misclassification

Defining worker status is difficult

Courts use a variety of legal tests to determine employee status

- Each of these tests requires analysis of a number of factors

- The tests differ by agency, by court, by state, and sometimes by context

- There are three main tests that are used to determine classification

The common law agency test

- The "right to control" forms the heart of the common law agency test.

- A number of factors are weighed:

- Most legal classification tests include analysis of the amount of control exerted over the employee

- This test arose out of the need to define when an employer had vicarious liability for the tortious acts of its agents

- The NLRA is required to use the common law agency test

Case discussion: NLRB v. Friendly Cab Co., *512 F.3d 1090 (9th Cir. 2008)*

Case discussion: Estrada v Fedex Ground Package System, Inc., *154 Cal App 4th 1 (2d Dist 2007)*

The IRS test

- Because it is charged with enforcement of wage withholding, classification of workers is important to the IRS

- The IRS originally used 20 factors

- The IRS later modified the test, by grouping the twenty factors into three categories:

- behavioral control,

- financial control, and

- type of relationship

- The IRS Voluntary Compliance Settlement Program is of little use to an employer

The economic reality test

- The economic reality test focuses on financial considerations

- Worker status is not based on the work itself, but on the financial reality that accompanies the work

- The economic reality test is used to classify workers under the

  - Fair Labor Standards Act,

  - Equal Pay Act of 1963,

  - Family and Medical Leave Act of 1993, and

  - Employee Polygraph Protection Act of 1988

Six factors comprise the economic reality test:

- The extent of the individual's investment in equipment and facilities

- The individual's opportunity for profit or loss

- The degree of control exercised by others over the individual's work

- The importance of the services to the alleged employer's business (i.e., whether the service performed is an integral part of the business)

- The permanency of the relationship between the work and the employer

- The skill required of the individual in performing the work.

The entrepreneurial aspect test

Case discussion: FedEx Home Delivery v. NLRB, *563 F.3d 492 (DC Cir. 2009)*

- In FedEx Home Delivery v. NLRB, the court used the common law test, but rejected the primacy of the right to control factor

- Instead, the court looked to the presence of entrepreneurship to determine independent contractor status

What to do about contingent or temporary workers?

The permatemp has become much more common in society

- A contingent worker is one whose job is temporary, sporadic, or differs in any way from the norm of full-time employment

- The temporary work force makes up 26% of American workers

What can temporary workers look forward to?

- No health insurance

- No sick days

- No paid vacation

- No retirement plan

- No severance pay

- Higher rates of depression and anxiety

Contingent workers could be entitled to some protection under employment laws

- Temporary workers may be excluded from corporate culture

- Temporary workers can be hired directly or through a staffing agency

- An employer may have several reasons why it hires through a staffing agency

An employee may have two employers called "joint employers"

- In the case of staffing firms, a worker may have TWO employers simultaneously

- Courts will examine a number of factors to determine which employer may be primarily liable

- The Browning-Ferris decision may have a huge impact on employment in the US

Conclusion

- The problem of employee classification is a constant problem

- Defining worker status is difficult

- Courts use a variety of legal tests to determine employee status

Proving discrimination: an overview of Title VII

Introduction

Setting

- The employment at will doctrine does not apply to cases of illegal discrimination

- Title VII of the Civil Rights Act of 1964 governs illegal discrimination in employment

- Despite laws against discrimination, employment litigation continues to grow

- Understanding Title VII is vital for all managers

Objective

- In this lecture, we look at what Title VII is, what it does, and how to prove an illegal discrimination case.

What does Title VII do?

Title VII protects against employment discrimination on the basis of

membership in protected classes

- Title VII protects five classes

- Title VII protects individuals against employment discrimination on the bases of race and color

- Title VII protects individuals against employment discrimination on the bases of national origin, sex, and religion

What does Title VII say?

- It shall be an unlawful employment practice for an employer

- to fail or refuse to hire or to discharge any individual, or otherwise to discriminate against any individual ... because of such individual's race, color, religion, sex, or national origin ...

Title VII's protections include the following

- Employment requirements must be uniformly and consistently applied

- Title VII prohibits offensive conduct that alters the conditions of employment

- Title VII prohibits discrimination in compensation

- Title VII prohibits physical segregation based on protected class

- Title VII protects employees who make a complaint from retaliation

Title VII does not apply to every employer

- An employer must have more than 15 employees

- Some institutions may be exempt

- Independent contractors are exempt

What was the reason for Title VII?

Title VII has its roots in the Fourteenth Amendment

- The amendment included a broad definition of citizenship

- The amendment guaranteed citizens the equal protection of the laws

- The amendment applied the Bill of Rights to the states

After the Civil War, Congress attempted to restructure the United States

- The Thirteenth Amendment prohibited slavery

- The Fourteenth Amendment guaranteed equal protection of the laws

- The Fifteenth Amendment attempted to protect political freedom

- The Civil Rights Act of 1866 attempted to protect social freedom

- Few provisions were made to protect economic freedom

Title VII permits an employee to sue in court for illegal discrimination

There are two different theories on which an employee can base his claim

of illegal discrimination

- Disparate treatment involves a policy or action that is discriminatory on its face

- Disparate impact involves policies that are neutral on their face, but which have a negative impact on a protected class

- Proving a claim under Title VII is a burden-shifting process

Disparate treatment is used for cases of discrimination against an individual rather than a group

- The employee must prove a prima facie case

- The prima facie case gives rise to a presumption of unlawful discrimination

- There are four elements to a prima facie case

- Plaintiff belongs to a protected class

- Plaintiff applied for and was qualified for the job

- Plaintiff was rejected for the position

- An employee outside of the protected class was selected for the position, or the employer continued to look for candidates

- The employer rebuts the prima facie case by showing a legitimate, non-discriminatory reason (LNDR)

- The plaintiff can prove the LNDR is actually a pretext to hide unlawful discrimination

An employer may establish a Bona Fide Occupational Qualification (BFOQ)

defense for certain disparate treatment cases

- BFOQ is available only for disparate treatment cases involving gender, religion and national origin

- A BFOQ is legalized discrimination

- The employer must show that this preference goes to the essence of its business

Case discussion: Wilson v. Southwest Airlines Company, *517 F. Supp 292 (ND Tex 1981)*

Disparate impact exists where an employer has a policy that is neutral

on its face but has a negative impact upon a protected category

- Disparate impact relates to groups of employees and not individuals

- Disparate impact regulates the use of screening devices

- Case discussion: Griggs v. Duke Power Co., *401 U.S. 424 (1971)*

There are several methods for establishing a prima facie case of

disparate impact

- The plaintiff must prove his prima facie case (generally using statistics)

- The plaintiff can show that the protected employees do not fare at least 80% as well as the majority under the policy

Disparate impact (80% rule)

- Example:

During 2013, 1500 applicants apply for a job requiring a test
1000 men applied and 500 women applied
100 women passed the test, while 300 men passed
100 passed/500 women = 0.2 (20%)
300 passed/1000 men = 0.3 (30%)
0.2/0.3 = 66%

- Result:

  - Because the percentage is LESS than 80%, disparate impact seems to exist.

- Burden now shifts to Defendant employer

- Nonscored objective criteria can also create disparate impact

- Subjective criteria may be subject to disparate impact analysis too

After the plaintiff makes a prima facie case, the burden shifts to the employer

- The employer rebuts by attacking the plaintiff's statistics

- The employer can also rebut by establishing that the screening device is a business necessity

- The plaintiff can rebut by proving that there is a less discriminatory alternative

Title VII provides remedies for violation of the statute

Historically, Title VII provided only equitable remedies

- The statute provides for equitable remedies:

- Back pay, for up to two years

- Front pay, if reinstatement is not possible

- Reinstatement, if feasible

- Retroactive seniority

- Injunctive relief

- Attorney fees

- The Civil Rights Act of 1991 provided the recovery of compensatory damages and punitive damages

- Punitive damages are not recoverable in a disparate impact case

- The Civil Rights Act of 1991 also added the right to a jury trial

Conclusion

- Title VII protects against employment discrimination

- Disparate treatment is used for cases of discrimination against an individual rather than a group

- Disparate impact focuses on the negative impact of policies which are neutral on their face

- Title VII provides equitable and legal remedies

The hiring process

Introduction

Setting

- Legal issues often arise during the hiring process

- The hiring process is composed of recruitment, information gathering, and testing before employment

- The business manager who neglects this area may expose his company to liability

Objective

- In this lecture, we study the legal implications of three aspects of the hiring process

Employers may stumble over legal issues in recruitment

Recruitment is regulated by both statutes and common law

- The law gives employers leeway in connection with their recruitment practices

- Employers may discriminate, as long as it is not based on membership in one of the protected classes

Federal and state statutes govern the recruitment process

- What federal statutes govern recruitment?

- Title VII of the Civil Rights Act of 1964

- Americans with Disabilities Act

- Age Discrimination in Employment Act

- Immigration Reform and Control Act of 1986

The common law regulates recruitment through the law of misrepresentation and fraud

- Employers may become legally responsible to employees for false statements

- These situations often involve comments made about job terms or the company's current financial condition

- Misrepresentations could also involve statements about the employee's continuing job security, promotions, or benefits

- The misrepresentation need not actually be a false statement--a false impression may be enough

- An employer's silence may constitute misrepresentation

- Fraud in recruitment occurs when misstatements are used to discourage potential applicants from pursuing positions

Common recruitment techniques could lead to a claim of employment discrimination

- Advertisements

- Word-of-mouth recruiting

- Nepotism

- Promoting from within

- Venue recruiting

- Walk-in applicants

- Neutral solicitation

- There are concerns with the collection of resumes

Information gathering and selection are also potential trouble areas

During the application process, information is gathered that is designed to screen out applicants

- Appropriate questions are business-related and used for a nondiscriminatory purpose

- Only a few questions are strictly prohibited

- Some questions are not prohibited but are dangerous

- Even use of a common employment application can result in potential liability

An employer may be liable for negligent hiring

- An employer should verify the qualifications of the applicant

- Try to insure that there is no undiscovered information

- An employer must exercise reasonable care in hiring applicants who may pose a risk to others

There may be potential liability for providing references

- In recent years, many employers have grown wary of the risk involved in responding to reference inquiries

- Employers may be liable for defamation

- Employers may be liable for negligent misrepresentation

- Some states have provided immunity for reference responses

- There is no immunity for an employer who gives a negative reference in retaliation for a Title VII claim

Testing is the third part of the hiring process

Pre-employment testing carries risk

- Pre-employment testing has become standard in the selection process

- Does the test accurately test for the characteristics sought?

Testing in the work place has taken two forms

- Testing for eligibility

- Tests for ineligibility

Legality of eligibility testing

- There are Title VII implications to testing

- Certain tests may have a disparate impact upon members of a protected class

- When do decisions based on disparate impact become disparate treatment?

- Case discussion: Ricci v. DeStefano, *129 S. Ct. 2658 (2009)*

If a test has been professionally developed and validated, Title VII does not prohibit its use

- An employer must establish that the test is a business necessity, as well as predictive of job performance

- Even where these two requirements have been satisfied, the test may be challenged if a less discriminatory alternative exists

There are other forms of eligibility testing

- Integrity and personality testing have become more predominant

- Physical ability tests may be administered to applicants

- Many employers require pre-employment, post-offer medical tests

Testing for ineligibility may cause problems

- Why would an employer want to test for ineligibility?

- The employer may wish to reduce workplace injury

- An employer may use to tests in order to predict employee performance

- Testing can reduce the employer's financial responsibility to the workers' compensation system

Under most circumstances, employers may test applicants

- Private testing does not generally raise constitutional implications

- State statutes may establish private sector requirements for workplace testing

- Private sector testing may result in common law invasion of privacy

- Workers may claim reckless or negligent infliction of emotional distress

- An employee may have a claim for defamation

There are other problems with ineligibility testing

- Polygraphs are notoriously unreliable (and possibly illegal)

- Drug and alcohol tests are routinely given

- Case discussion: National Treasury Employees Union v. Von Raab, *489 U.S. 656 (1989).*

- Genetic testing is the next area to watch

Conclusion

- Recruitment of employees is regulated by both statutes and the common law

- There are multiple legal issues related to information gathering and selection

- Testing is the third part of the hiring process

Race and color discrimination

Introduction

Setting

- The drafters of the Civil Rights Act of 1964 were most concerned with racial discrimination

- No adequate definition of race exists

- The concept of race is a recent invention

- Despite years of effort, the problems of racial discrimination remain

Objective

- In this lecture, we look at Title VII's treatment of racial discrimination

Title VII was aimed at racial discrimination

Title VII makes racial discrimination illegal

- It shall be an unlawful employment practice for an employer:

- to fail or refuse to hire or to discharge any individual, or otherwise to discriminate against any individual with respect to his compensation, terms, conditions, or privileges of employment, because of such individual's race, color …

A background to Title VII

- History and its effects account for much of today's race discrimination

- Slavery lasted for over 200 years as an integral part of American life

- A number of legal structures institutionalized race

The Reconstruction era Civil Rights Act discouraged racial discrimination

- The 1866 Civil Rights Act included three sections related to employment

- The Reconstruction Era acts remain relevant today.

- Actions under the Reconstruction Era acts must be brought by the employee suing the employer in court

42 U.S.C. Section 1981 is arguably the most important section

- §1981 guarantees equal rights under the law to make and enforce contracts

- The Civil Rights Act of 1991 overturned the Patterson decision

42 U.S.C. Section 1983 protects against discrimination involving state action

- §1983 protects citizens for deprivation of their Constitutional rights under color of state law

- Section 1983 applies to public employers and to those associated with a governmental entity

- Case discussion: Jett v. Dallas Independent School District *491 U.S. 701 (1989)*

42 U.S.C. Section 1985 is aimed at conspiracies

- §1985 prohibits a conspiracy to interfere with Civil Rights

- §1985 addresses conspiracies to interfere with or deprive the civil rights of others

- Case discussion: Mississippi Burning

Title VII covers two areas: racial discrimination and racial harassment

The notion of race has expanded

- The EEOC uses different factors to determine race

- EEOC guidelines to determine race

  - Ancestry

- Physical characteristics

- Race-linked illness

- Culture

- Perception

- Association

Case discussion: Alonzo v. Chase Manhattan Bank, NA, *25 F. Supp. 2d 455 (S.D.N.Y. 1998)*

Title VII prohibits discrimination on the basis of race

- Title VII places obligations on employers

- The employer must ensure that every employee has an equal opportunity

- Employers must be vigilant to guard against overt and subtle manifestations of race discrimination

A case of racial discrimination may be established by disparate treatment or disparate impact

- Disparate treatment may be shown by direct or indirect evidence of discrimination

- Disparate impact may be more difficult to discern

- Race cannot be used as a bona fide occupational qualification.

A word about color

- Case discussion: Walker v. Secretary of the Treasury, Internal Revenue Service *742 F. Supp. 670 (N.D. Ga. 1990)*

- Recognizing race discrimination may be an issue

- The latest EEOC statistics indicate that race remains the most frequent type of claim filed with the agency.

There are other issues related to racial discrimination

An employer may be liable for racial harassment

- To hold an employer liable for racial harassment, the employee must show that the harassment was:

- Unwelcome

- Based on race

- So severe or pervasive that it altered the conditions of employment and created an abusive environment

Proper management strategies can avoid race claims

- Keep certain general considerations in mind

- Race discrimination may occur against any group and is equally prohibited under Title VII

- Believe that race discrimination occurs and be wiling to acknowledge it when it is alleged

- Make sure there is a top-down message that the workplace will not tolerate race discrimination in any form

- Don't shy away from discussing race when the issues arises.

- Provide a positive, non-threatening, constructive forum for the discussion of racial issues.

- When an employee reports race discrimination, don't tell the employee he or she must be mistaken.

- Be willing to treat the matter as a misunderstanding if it is clear that is what has taken place

- Offer training in racial awareness and sensitivity.

- Constantly monitor workplace hiring, termination, training, promotion, raises, and discipline to ensure that they are fair and even-handed

Conclusion

- Title VII was aimed primarily at racial discrimination

- Title VII covers two areas: racial discrimination and racial harassment

- Proper management strategies can avoid claims

Sex discrimination

Introduction

Setting

- Sex discrimination differs from race discrimination

- Protection against discrimination on the basis of sex was a last-minute addition to Title VII

- Courts have struggled with balancing societal interests

- Gender-related claims continue to increase

Objective

- In this lecture, we study the basics of sex discrimination

Title VII prohibits discrimination in employment based on sex

Sex-based differences in the workplace continue

- The law prohibits discrimination on the basis of sex in employment practices

- Case discussion: Wedow v. City of Kansas City, Missouri, *442 F. 3d 661 (8th Cir. 2006)*

- Sometimes policies may not appear illegal or be intended for illegal purposes, but ...

- Case discussion: Dothard v. Rawlinson, *433 U.S. 321 (1977)*

Employers may only select employees based on their sex if a particular

gender is a bona fide occupational qualification (BFOQ)

- Gender may be used as a bona fide occupational qualification under certain limited circumstances

- Attempts to use a gender based BFOQ rarely succeed

Case discussion: Diaz v. Pan American, *311 F.Supp. 559 (S.D. FL 1970)*

A BFOQ may only be justified by business necessity and not business

convenience

- BFOQs may be supported by community standards of morality or propriety

- Sex stereotyping is another form of gender discrimination

- Employers may not make employment decisions on the basis of stereotypes

Case discussion: Price Waterhouse v. Hopkins, *490 U.S. 228 (1989)*

- The mixed-motive problem: An illegal factor cannot be considered in making an employment decision

Sex discrimination may appear in different ways

Gender-plus discrimination is a form of sex discrimination

- Gender-plus discrimination involves the placing of additional requirements on employees of a certain sex

- Employers may hire women in general but not hire women with certain other factors

Case discussion: Phillips v. Martin Marietta Corp., *400 U.S. 542 (1971)*

Grooming codes raise issues of sex discrimination

- Workplace grooming codes may relate to sex stereotyping

- Courts give employers a great deal of leeway to determine workplace dress code

Case discussion: Harper v. Blockbuster Entertainment Corporation, *139 F. 3d 1385 (11th Cir. 1998)*

- Not every difference in dress codes based upon gender is illegal

Case discussion: Jespersen v. Harrah's Operating Co., *444 F. 3d 1104 (9th Cir. 2006)*

Customer or employee preferences raise issues of sex discrimination

- Title VII does not permit the employer to consider customer or employee preferences

- The Civil Rights Act of 1991 extended Title VII to U.S. citizens employed by American companies outside the United States

The EEOC has determined that sexual orientation discrimination is illegal discrimination because of sex

- Sexual orientation discrimination is by its nature based on sex

- There are three reasons for this determination

- sexual orientation discrimination necessarily involves treating workers less favorably because of their sex because sexual orientation as a concept cannot be understood without reference to sex;

- sexual orientation discrimination is rooted in non-compliance with sex stereotypes and gender norms, and employment decisions based in such stereotypes and norms have long been found to be prohibited sex discrimination under Title VII; and

- sexual orientation discrimination punishes workers because of their close personal association with members of a particular sex

- In 2016, the EEOC filed its first workplace sexual harassment cases based on sexual orientation

The Equal Pay Act mandates equal pay for equal work

What is equal work?

- Equal work under the EPA need only be substantially equivalent

Equal work means equal effort, equal skills, and equal responsibility

- Equal effort involves substantially equivalent physical or mental exertion needed for performance of the jobs

- Equal skill includes substantially equivalent experience, training, education, and ability

- Equal responsibility includes a substantially equivalent degree of accountability

- Working conditions include the physical surroundings and hazards involved in a job

There are defenses to liability under the Equal Pay Act

- Pay differentials could result from

- seniority system

- Seniority systems must be bona fide and apply equally to all employees

- merit pay system

  - Merit pay systems must consist of a formal system using objective determination of employees' merit

- productivity-pay system

- or a "factor other than sex"

  - The factor other than sex is a broad defense

- Case discussion: Laffey v. Northwest Airlines, *567 F. 2d 429 (1976)*

The EEOC enforces the Equal Pay Act

- A party may sue under the Equal Pay Act separately

- Remedies under the EPA include back pay and an equal amount as liquidated damages

- Case discussion: Ledbetter v. Goodyear Tire & Rubber Co., *550 U.S. 618 (2007)*

- The Lilly Ledbetter Fair Pay Act of 2009 changed the statute of limitations for equal pay claims

Conclusion

- Title VII prohibits discrimination in employment based on sex

- Gender discrimination may appear in different ways

- The Equal Pay Act prohibits sex-based pay differentials between men and women performing substantially equivalent work

Sexual harassment

Introduction

Setting

- Sexual harassment has received a good deal of attention since the 1990s

- Sexual harassment costs employers millions of dollars

- Sexual harassment constitutes a form of sex discrimination

- Sexual harassment violates Title VII of the 1964 Civil Rights Act

Objective

- In this lecture, we examine Title VII and its prohibition of sexual harassment

The law recognizes two forms of sexual harassment

Sexual harassment law is not designed to eliminate sexuality in the workplace

- The EEOC issued guidelines to use to help determine when sexual harassment occurs

- The intent of sexual harassment law is not that the workplace become devoid of sexuality

- Consensual relationships are not forbidden and employees may date

- It becomes a problem when the activity directed toward an employee is unwelcome

- Sexual harassment imposes terms or conditions different for one sex than the other

There are two theories of liability for sexual harassment claims

- Quid pro quo implies "this for that"

- Hostile environment is similar to other forms of harassment under Title VII

Quid pro quo sexual harassment

Quid pro quo sexual harassment involves a demand for sexual activity in exchange for workplace benefits

- Quid pro quo sexual harassment is the most obvious form of harassment

- Quid pro quo harassment is often accompanied by a paper trail

A prima facie case of quid pro quo sexual harassment requires three elements

- Prima facie case of quid pro quo sexual harassment

- Unwelcome sexual advances

- Submission was a term or condition of employment

- Submission or rejection was used as the basis for an employment decision

A prima facie case for quid pro quo sexual harassment could be summarized as:

- Workplace benefit promised, given to, or withheld from harassee by harasser

- In exchange for sexual activity by harassee

- Complainant must establish that conduct was unwelcome

Case discussion: Bryson v. Chicago State University, *96 F. 3d 912 (1996)*

Hostile environment sexual harassment

A prima facie case of hostile environment sexual harassment requires the following

- A prima facie case for hostile work environment sexual harassment

    - He or she suffered intentional discrimination because of his/her sex.

    - The discrimination was pervasive and severe.

    - The discrimination detrimentally affected him or her.

    - The discrimination would detrimentally affect a reasonable person of the same sex.

Case discussion: Meritor Savings Bank, FSB v. Vinson, *477 U.S. 57 (1986)*

Employers are often confused about what conduct rises to the level of hostile environment

- A finding of hostile environment sexual harassment requires more than occasional comments

- Not all conduct, even if it is offensive, will be found to create a hostile environment

- Certain types of conduct that will create a hostile environment

The plaintiff must show unwelcome activity

- The basis of hostile environment sexual harassment actions is unwanted activity

- If the activity is wanted or welcome by the complainant, there is no sexual harassment

- Courts can examine both direct and indirect actions to determine whether the activity was welcome

The standard of hostile work environment is not always clear

Case discussion: Rabidue v. Osceola Refining Co., *805 F. 2d 611 (6th Cir. 1986)*

- The Supreme Court clarified the hostile work environment standard

- Men can be the victim of sexual harassment

An abusive working environment requires severe or pervasive intimidation, ridicule, or insult

- Courts must often determine whether the harassing activity was severe and pervasive enough

- The more frequent the occurrences, the more likely that the severe and pervasive requirement will be met

- Case discussion: Ross v. Double Diamond, Inc., *672 F. Supp. 261 (N.D. Tx. 1987)*

Courts have confronted the problem of perspective: Which perspective is used to determine severity?

- The determination was historically based upon the reasonable person standard

- Courts have increasingly used the reasonable victim standard

Case discussion: Ellison v. Brady, *924 F. 2d 872 (9th Cir. 1991)*

- Courts look to the perspective of a reasonable person in the plaintiff's position

Case discussion: Oncale v. Sundowner Offshore Services, Inc., *523 U.S. 75 (1998)*

The distinctions between quid pro quo and hostile work environment are not always clear

Case discussion: Showalter v. Allison Reed Group, Inc., *767 F. Supp. 1205 (D.C. RI 1991)*

Sexual harassment doesn't have to be about sexual activity

- While the harassment of the employee must be based upon gender, it need not involve sexual activity

- A hostile environment may be displayed through the use of derogatory terms

- Employers should not dismiss a harassment complaint simply because it does not mention sexual activity

An employer may have liability for sexual harassment

Courts have wrestled with the with the issue of employer liability for sexual harassment

- Courts have struggled to define the relevant standards of employer liability

- Employers are liable when either their supervisors or agents create a hostile environment

- In general, an employer is also liable if it

  - knew or should have known of the activity and

  - failed to take appropriate corrective action

- Employers are usually deemed to know of sexual harassment if it is:

  - openly practiced in the workplace

  - well-known among employees

- brought to the employer's notice by a victim's filing a charge

Companies that want to manage their risk prudently must act before a problem occurs

- Companies need a comprehensive, detailed written policy on sexual harassment

- Once a company develops a sexual harassment policy, it should circulate it widely

- A company should have a grievance procedure

- A company must enforce its policy quickly, consistently, and aggressively

An employer can be liable for harassment by supervisors, coworkers, or third parties

- Employer liability may depend on whether there has been a tangible action

Supervisor toward employee (tangible employment action)

- An employer is strictly liable for the tangible acts of its supervisors

- An employer has no defense where there is a tangible act by a supervisor

- Therefore, in a quid pro quo case, the employer is always liable for the acts of its employee

Supervisor toward employee (no tangible employment action)

- If there is no tangible employment act by a supervisor, the employer is not strictly liable

- Case discussion: Burlington Industries, Inc. v. Ellerth, *524 U.S. 742 (1998)*

- An employer can be vicariously liable if the actions by the supervisor constitute severe or pervasive sexual harassment

The employer can evade liability by proving an affirmative defense

- The employer must prove that

- the employer exercised reasonable care to prevent or correct promptly any such sexual harassment, and

- the employee unreasonably failed to take advantage of any preventative or corrective opportunities provided by the employer or to avoid harm otherwise.

Coworker harassment

- The employer is liable

- if the employer knew or should have known of the acts of the harasser and

- took no immediate corrective action

Third party harassment of employee

- In general, the employer is liable

- if the employer knew or should have known of the acts of the harasser and

- took no immediate corrective action

There are ways for employers to avoid liability for sexual harassment claims

An employer must determine the truth of the allegations

- Managers may have difficulty have with addressing sexual harassment complaints

- Appropriate investigation will provide the employer a basis upon which to decide and how to respond

- The complainant must be informed of certain items

The employer must take immediate and appropriate corrective action to remedy sexual harassment

- The most appropriate remedy depends upon the facts

- The remedy must be calculated to stop the harassment and not have the effect of punishing the victim

Victims of sexual harassment may also seek other civil remedies

- Tort law provides for remedies for certain acts of sexual harassment

- A number of torts can occur as a result of sexual harassment

    - Assault

    - Battery

    - Intentional infliction of emotional distress

    - False imprisonment

    - Tortious interference with contract

- An employer may have indirect or direct liability under a tort theory

- Harassment could even be the basis for criminal prosecution

Conclusion

- The law recognizes two forms of sexual harassment

- An employer may have liability for sexual harassment

- There are other considerations in regard to sexual harassment claims

National origin discrimination

Introduction

Setting

- There are three trends in cases alleging national origin discrimination

- National origin claims are increasingly brought as race claims

- Language claims are brought as national origin claims

- National origin claims more frequently allege harassment

Objective

- In this lecture, we examine national origin discrimination under Title VII

Title VII prohibits employers from discriminating against employees based upon the national origin of the employee

Title VII does not define 'national origin'

- The Supreme Court has interpreted 'national origin' to refer to geography

- The EEOC says that employment discrimination against a national origin group includes discrimination based on:

- Ethnicity

- Physical, linguistic, or cultural traits

- Perception

- Courts have differed on whether national origin claims can be brought as § 1981 claims

National origin discrimination cases are resolved in the standard manner

- The plaintiff must first make the prima facie case

- The plaintiff must establish

- that she belongs to a protected group;

- that she was qualified for her position;

- that she suffered an adverse employment action or was denied an employment benefit; and

- that other similarly-situated employees, not in her protected class, were more favorably treated

- The defendant employer responds with either LNDR or BFOQ

- National origin can be a bona fide occupational qualification

- Customer preference is never a justification for a discriminatory practice

Discrimination can occur when the victim and the person who inflicted the discrimination are of the same national origin

- Case discussion: Kang v. U. Lim America, Inc., *296 F.3d 810 (9th Cir. 2002)*

Language issues may reveal discrimination based on national origin

Accent discrimination may be an issue

- The test is whether the accent materially interferes with the ability to perform job duties

- There is a difference between a discernible foreign accent and one that interferes with communication skills

- An employer may only base an employment decision on accent if

  - effective oral communication in English is required to perform job duties and

  - the individual's foreign accent materially interferes with his or her ability to communicate orally in English

- Case discussion: Carino v University of Oklahoma, *750 F. 2d 815 (10th Cir. 1984)*

Fluency requirements may indicate national origin discrimination

- A fluency requirement is permissible only if required for the effective performance of the position for which it is imposed

- The employer should not require a greater degree of fluency than is necessary for the relevant position

- Fluency requirements may lead to a hostile environment claim

- Foreign language fluency may be a requirement

English-Only rules may indicate national origin discrimination

- Some employers have instituted policies prohibiting communication in languages other than English

- An English-only rule may only be adopted for nondiscriminatory reasons

- An English-only rule is justified by business necessity if it is needed for an employer to operate safely or efficiently

Case discussion: Garcia v. Spun Steak Co., *998 F. 2d 1480 (9th Cir. 1993)*

The following issues should be addressed whenever the employer seeks to establish an English-only policy:

- Business necessity

- Supervisory concerns

- Workplace safety

- Productivity

Title VII provides a remedy for harassment based on national origin

- Harassment is one of the most common claims raised in national origin charges filed with the EEOC

- The last decade saw an increase in the number of private sector national origin harassment charges filed with the EEOC

- Thirty percent of all private sector national origin charges included a harassment claim

Title VII prohibits harassment on the basis of national origin

Title VII provides a remedy for harassment based on national origin

- It is unlawful to harass a person because of his or her national origin

- Harassment is one of the most common claims raised in national origin charges filed with the EEOC

- The last decade saw an increase in the number of private sector national origin harassment charges filed with the EEOC

- Thirty percent of all private sector national origin charges included a harassment claim

National origin harassment violates Title VII

- Harassment because of national origin, including ethnic slurs and other verbal or physical conduct, is discriminatory if the conduct:

- Creates or is intended to create an intimidating, hostile, offensive working environment;

- Unreasonably interferes with work performance; or

- Otherwise adversely affects an individual's employment opportunities.

Employers may be liable for harassment:

- By their supervisors, whether or not they knew of its occurrence

- By employees and nonemployees if they knew or should have known of the conduct and did not take steps to correct it

Employers are responsible for all forms of unlawful harassment

- by supervisors if the harassment culminates in a tangible employment action

- If no tangible employment action results, the employer may be able to avoid liability or limit damages by establishing an affirmative defense

To prevent harassment in the workplace, and to support an affirmative defense to a claim of harassment, employers should:

- Establish anti-harassment policies and complaint procedures

- Make sure the policies and procedures are clearly communicated to all employees; and

- Train supervisors in preventing harassment, responding to harassment complaints, and avoiding post-complaint retaliation.

Conclusion

- Title VII prohibits any employment decision based on national origin

- Title VII provides a remedy for harassment based on national origin

- National origin claims may involve language issues

Age discrimination

Introduction

Setting

- American culture values youth

- By 2030 the number of workers 65 and over will more than double

- Incorporating older workers will be a challenge for employers in the future

- Age discrimination will be the next major area of conflict

Objective

- In this lecture, we examine the Age Discrimination in Employment Act

The Age Discrimination in Employment Act regulates age discrimination

There are many misperceptions in the marketplace regarding older workers

- Statistics show that older workers are more reliable, harder working, more committed and have less absenteeism than younger workers

- Nevertheless, many in the workplace don't see it that way

- Many employers feel older employees may be more expensive to retain

    - Examples of when age discrimination can occur in the workplace:

    - Hiring, forced retirement, firing

    - Job advertisements and recruitment

    - Compensation, pay, regular and fringe benefits

    - Waivers of the right to sue in exchange for severance pay

In 1967, Congress enacted the Age Discrimination in Employment Act ("ADEA")

- The statute was designed to promote employment of older persons on the basis of ability

- The law forbids discrimination when it comes to any aspect of employment

- Age discrimination involves treating an applicant or employee less favorably because of age

The Act applies to employment by public and private employers with more than 20 employees

- The Act protects employees over forty years old from discrimination

- It does not protect workers under the age of forty

- There is no claim for "reverse discrimination" under the ADEA

- It is not illegal for an employer to favor an older worker over a younger one

- Discrimination can occur when the victim and the person who discriminated are both over 40

There are similarities and differences between ADEA and Title VII

- Both are enforced by the EEOC, as well as through private actions

- Discrimination based on age is more difficult to establish than a Title VII claim

- Intent must be proved for an age discrimination claim

- The ADEA allows employers greater latitude than Title VII in the reasons for an adverse employment decision

ADEA Plaintiffs may prove their case through either disparate treatment or disparate impact

The Employee's Prima Facie Case: Disparate Treatment

- The age discrimination prima facie case is similar to Title VII

- The plaintiff must prove that she was in the protected class

- She must have suffered an adverse employment action

- The plaintiff was qualified for the position

- The plaintiff must show that he was treated differently than a younger worker

- The mixed-motive analysis is not relevant to an ADEA age discrimination claim

- Case discussion: Gross v. FBL Financial Services, *129 S. Ct. 2343 (2009)*

If the employee makes a prima facie case, the burden of proof shifts to the employer

- The employer may establish a legitimate nondiscriminatory reason for its actions

- The ADEA provides for a bona fide occupational qualification defense

- Age is one of the most consistently applied BFOQs

- The employer's proof of a bona fide occupational qualification under the ADEA is different than Title VII

- Title VII requires that the employer demonstrate that

- the essence of the business requires the exclusion of the members of a protected class

- all or substantially all of the members of that class are unable to perform adequately in the position in question

Under the ADEA, the employer must prove

- The age limit is reasonably necessary to the essence of the employer's business; and either

- All or substantially all of the individuals over that age are unable to perform the job's requirements adequately; or

- Some of the individuals over that age possess a disqualifying trait that cannot be ascertained except by reference to age

- This third element allows an employer to exclude older workers from a position that may be safe to some older workers

- Case discussion: Western Air Lines, Inc. v. Criswell, *472 U.S. 400 (1985)*

- Congress has prohibited mandatory retirement ages for most workers

Employee's Prima Facie Case: Circumstances Involving Claims of Disparate Impact

- An ADEA plaintiff may establish a claim based on disparate impact

- Courts view statistical based disparate impact claims with skepticism

- Disparate impact claims filed under the ADEA require proof of discriminatory motive

An employer's defense in an ADEA disparate impact case is likely to be RFOA

- A discriminatory policy is valid if based on a reasonable factor other than age (RFOA)

- The RFOA defense is different than the business necessity defense

- Reasonable factors other than age include economic concerns and seniority plans

Employer economic concerns may justify adverse action against older workers

- It is likely to be more expensive to maintain older workers than younger

- An objective standard must be used in determining terminations

- Courts disfavor the economic justification for the termination of older workers

- These terminations are generally legal:

    - reductions in force (RIF)

    - bankruptcy

    - Other legitimate business reasons

Case discussion: Hazen Paper Co. v. Biggins, *113 S.Ct. 1701 (1993)*

- We have little guidance on legal effect of the correlation between age and compensation

Employee's Response: Proof of Pretext

- The employee responds by establishing that the reason or defense is pretextual

- An employee can show pretext in a number of ways

Case discussion: Pottenger v. Potlatch Corp., *329 F. 3d 740 (9th Cir. 2003)*

Age discrimination raises other issues for management

Employers often encourage older workers to waive their ADEA rights

- The Older Workers Benefit Protection Act ("OWBPA") modified the ADEA

- The OWBPA concerns the legality and enforceability of early retirement incentive programs

- Employers must meet the requirements of the OWBPA in formulating waivers

- Case discussion: Oubre v. Entergy Operations, Inc, *118 S.Ct. 838 (1998)*

Remedies for age discrimination are limited

- Employees may receive front pay or back pay

- Compensation for pain and suffering is generally not available under the ADEA

- Forms of equitable relief include

  - Reinstatement

  - Promotions or injunctions

Conclusion

- The Age Discrimination in Employment Act regulates age discrimination

- Plaintiffs may prove their case through either disparate treatment or disparate impact

- Age discrimination raises other issues for management

Religious discrimination

Introduction

Setting

- Religious discrimination is different than other forms of discrimination prohibited by Title VII

- Religion is a set of beliefs, not a physical characteristic

- The law has recognized the difference in religious discrimination

- Religious discrimination can serve as a stumbling block for employers

Objective

- In this lecture, we examine Title VII's protection against religious discrimination

Title VII bans discrimination on the basis of religion

The role of religion in American life

- Many settlers in the early United States were religious dissenters

- The Second Great Awakening increased religion's role in political affairs

- Theory of manifest destiny further integrated religion into American politics

Religious organizations are generally exempt from the prohibitions in Title VII

Case discussion: <u>Corporation of the Presiding Bishop of the Church of Jesus Christ of Latter-day Saints v. Amos, 483 U.S. 327 (1987)</u>

Case discussion: Spencer v. World Vision, Inc, *633 F. 3d 723 (9th Cir. 2010)*

- The ministerial exemption prevents interference with church employment

Case discussion: McClure v. Salvation Army, *460 F. 2d 553 (5th Cir. 1972)*

Religion can serve as a BFOQ

- Title VII permits religion to be a bona fide occupational qualification

- Title VII specifically permits educational institutions to employ those of a particular religion

Case discussion: Pime v. Loyola University of Chicago, *803 F. 2d 351 (7th Cir. 1986)*

Identification of sincerely held beliefs can be problematic

"Religion? That's not a religion!"

- Originally, Title VII did not define religion

- Congress amended the statute in 1972 to say religion is:

  - " … all aspects of religious observance and practice, as well as belief …"

- Religious status is based on two considerations

  - whether the belief is closely held

  - whether it takes the place of religion in the employee's life

- The religious belief need not be a belief in a religious deity as we generally know it

- The employer cannot question the sincerity of the belief merely because it appears to be unorthodox

- The employer cannot take an adverse employment action against the employee if the employer objects to the belief

Case discussion: Peterson v. Wilmur Communs., Inc., *205 F. Supp. 2d 1014 (E.D. Wisc. 2002)*

Personal preferences can be distinguished from religious beliefs

- Employees will sometimes request an accommodation for a personal preference in exercising their religion

Case discussion: Brown v. Pena, *441 F. Supp. 1382 (D.C. Fla. 1997)*

- An employee may not transmute political or other nonreligious views into a claim of a sincerely held religious belief

Proving a case of religious discrimination is different because of the duty to accommodate

- The law provides two means of bringing a claim for religious discrimination

- An employee can bring a claim that the employer treated him differently because of religion

- An employee can bring a claim that the employer failed to accommodate his religion

Disparate treatment analysis requires different treatment because of religion

- The prima facie case of disparate treatment based on religion is the same as for other Title VII classes

Case discussion: Campos v. City of Blue Springs, *289 F. 3d 546 (8th Cir. 2002)*

- The employer defends by citing LNDR or BFOQ

Case discussion: Sharon Adelman Reyes v. St. Xavier University, *500 F. 3d 662 (7th Cir. 2007)*

Religious discrimination is distinguished by the concept of reasonable accommodation

There is not an absolute prohibition against religious discrimination

- There is no reasonable accommodation requirement for race, gender, color or national origin
- The employer and employee each have a duty to accommodate

An employee asserting a claim of religious discrimination for failure to accommodate must first establish a prima facie case

- The employee must establish that
- he has a bona fide religious belief that conflicts with an employment requirement;
- he informed the employer of this belief and requested an accommodation of it; and
- he was disciplined or discharged for failing to comply with the conflicting employment requirement.

- An employer may defend by

- showing that it offered the employee "reasonable accommodation" or

- that the accommodation sought cannot be accomplished without undue burden

Once an employer is aware of a religious conflict, the employer must make a good faith attempt to accommodate the conflict

- An employer is only required to accommodate a religious practice to the extent that it does not cause an undue hardship

- An employer can discriminate against an employee for religious reasons if to not do so causes the employer undue hardship

- If no accommodation can be worked out without undue hardship on the part of the employer, the employer has fulfilled its Title VII duty

Case discussion: Goldman v. Weinberger, *475 U.S. 503 (1986)*

An employer does not have to accommodate if it imposes undue hardship

- What constitutes undue hardship also varies from situation to situation

- The accommodation the employer rejects as undue hardship may not be a mere inconvenience to the employer

- Relevant factors

    - the nature of the employer's workplace

    - the type of job needing accommodation

    - the cost of the accommodation

    - the willingness of other employees to assist in the accommodation

    - the possibility of transfer of the employee and its effects

    - what is done by similarly situated employers

    - the number of employees available for accommodation

    - the burden of accommodation upon the union

The employee's obligation to cooperate does not arise until the employer shows it has taken some initial steps

- The employee must assist in the attempted accommodation

Case discussion: Wilson v. U.S. West Communications, *58 F. 3d 1337 (8th Cir. 1995)*

Case discussion: Cloutier v. Costco Wholesale Corp, *390 F. 3d 126 (1st Cir. 2004).*

If accommodation is not possible, the employer can discriminate against an employee on the basis of religion

- Every case is fact-dependent and it is hard to make a general rule

Case discussion: Williams v. Southern Union Gas Co., *529 F. 2d 483 (10th Cir. 1976)*

- An employer need not accommodate everything an employee wishes to do because it is related to the employee's religion

Case discussion: Chalmers v. Tulon Company of Richmond, *101 F. 3d 1012 (1996) (4th Cir. 1996)*

An employer may be liable for religious harassment

Harassment on the basis of religion is illegal under Title VII

- It is often non-religious employees who allege they are being harassed by religious employees

- How much religious practice is acceptable in the workplace?

Case discussion: Peterson v. Hewlett-Packard Co., *358 F. 3d 599 (9th Cir. 2004)*

Conclusion

- Title VII bans discrimination on the basis of religion

- Identification of sincerely held beliefs can be problematic

- Proving a case of religious discrimination is different because of the duty to accommodate

Affirmative action

Introduction

Setting

- Affirmative action is a controversial area of employment law

- There are many misconceptions about affirmative action

- Affirmative action involves an affirmative effort to make the workplace reflective of the population

- Affirmative action is rarely mandatory

Objective

- In this lecture, we examine affirmative action and its place in employment law

Sometimes businesses need to take more than a passive approach to equal employment opportunity

What is affirmative action and why do we need it?

- Affirmative action involves an intentional effort to include those traditionally excluded in the workplace

- Affirmative action programs are not required by Title VII

- Affirmative action must be based on a finding of discrimination, underrepresentation, or a manifest imbalance in the workplace

- The phrase "affirmative action" comes from Executive Order 11246

- "The contractor will take affirmative action to ensure that applicants are employed, and that employees are treated during employment, without regard to their race, color, religion, sex, or national origin ..."

Affirmative action has always been a limited remedy

- Affirmative action regulations do not apply to every business

- Affirmative action does not require quotas

Affirmative action arises in different ways

Affirmative action arises in three ways

- Affirmative action can arise from contractual obligations with the federal government

- Affirmative action can arise as part of a judicial remedy

- Affirmative action can arise through voluntary efforts of the employer

Affirmative Action under Executive Order 11246

- Affirmative action stems from Executive Order 11246

- This program is enforced by the Office of Federal Contract Compliance Programs (OFCCP)

- EO 11246 only applies to federal government contracts

Affirmative Action Plans are based on availability

- Based on the availability of women and minorities qualified for the particular job

- Factors used to determine availability:

- The percentage of minorities or women with requisite skills in the reasonable recruitment area

- The percentage of minorities or women among those promotable, transferable, and trainable within the contractor's organization

- A placement goal is not a quota

- The regulations also require corporate management compliance evaluations

Judicial Affirmative Action

- Affirmative action may be a remedy for a Title VII violation

- There are no specific requirements regarding a judicial affirmative action

Case discussion: Local 28, Sheet Metal Workers v. EEOC, *478 U.S. 421 (1986)*

Voluntary Affirmative Action

- An employer may take proactive measures to avoid discrimination claims

Case discussion: United Steelworkers of America, AFL-CIO v. Weber, *443 U.S. 193 (1979)*

- The employer may create a voluntary affirmative action plan

The Supreme Court has adopted a three-part test to determine if a voluntary affirmative action plan is valid

- **First:** The purposes of the plan must mirror the remedial purposes of Title VII to end discrimination

- **Second:** the voluntary affirmative action plan cannot "unnecessarily trammel" the interests of non-minority employees

- **Third:** the plan must be a temporary measure meant to eliminate imbalance and not to maintain a balance Case discussion: Taxman v. Board of Education, *91 F.3d 1547 (3d Cir. 1996)*

An affirmative action plan may not use quotas

Case discussion: Regents of the University of California v Bakke, *438 U.S. 265 (1978)*

- Such plans should not displace nonminority employees

Case discussion: Gratz v. Bollinger, *123 S.Ct. 2411 (U.S. 2003)*

- An affirmative action plan is different from a "diversity" plan

Case discussion: Hopwood v. Texas, *78 F. 3d 932 (5th Cir. 1996)*

Case discussion: Grutter v. Bollinger, *539 U.S. 306 (2003)*

Case discussion: Fisher v. University of Texas, *133 S.Ct. 2411 (2013)* and *579 US ___*

Reverse Discrimination

- Reverse discrimination is often considered the flip side of affirmative action

- Reverse discrimination accounts for only about 3 percent of charges filed with EEOC

Conclusion

- Businesses need to take more than a passive approach to equal employment opportunity

- Affirmative action arises in three ways

- Companies should be mindful of reverse discrimination issues

Disability discrimination

Introduction

Setting

- Disability discrimination is often a hidden form of discrimination

- Prior to legislation, employers consistently refused to hire individuals with disabilities

- Accommodating disabilities costs money

- Without regulation, employers were not willing to bear that burden

Objective

- In this lecture, we examine the Americans with Disabilities Act and its regulation of disability discrimination

The regulation of disability discrimination has a long history

Congress first addressed disability discrimination in 1973

- Congress enacted the Vocational Rehabilitation Act of 1973

- The VRA required federal contractors to take affirmative action to employ and promote qualified disabled individuals

The Americans with Disabilities Act became effective in 1992

- The impact of the ADA has been less than its advocates hoped for

- In 2008, Congress attempted to strengthen the ADA

- The ADA Amendment Act (ADAAA) was passed to clarify and broaden the definition of disability and increase the coverage of the ADA

The ADA protects the disabled from three types of barriers

- Intentional discrimination for reasons of social bias

- Neutral standards with disparate impact on the disabled

- Discrimination as a result of barriers to job performance

Proving the case for disability discrimination

The plaintiff must first make the prima facie case

- There are four elements to the prima facie case

- He or she is disabled

- He or she is otherwise qualified for the position

- The disability can be reasonably accommodated

- He or she suffered an adverse employment decision

"He or she is disabled"

- The ADA defines disability as

- a physical or mental impairment that substantially limits one or more of the major life activities of an individual;

- a record of having such impairment;

- or being regarded as having such an impairment.

- The definition of disability thus has three elements:

- impairment;

- major life activity; and

- substantial limitation

What is a "physical or mental impairment?"

- Impairment is a broad term

- Don't mistake diagnosis for disability

- Substantially limited" is the test for disability

The impairment must substantially limit one or more of major life activities

- Court decisions have attempted to define major life activity and substantially limited

- Positive effects of mitigating measures should not be considered in determining substantial limitation

"Major life activity" is not defined in the ADA

- Major life activities are activities that the average person can perform with little or no difficulty

- Having a record of an impairment may lead to a finding of disability

Case discussion: School Bd. of Nassau County v. Arline, *107 S.Ct. 1123 (1987)*

The ADA definition of "disability" includes perception of others

- A person may have a disability if his impairment is treated as such

- The ADAAA expanded the definition of "regarded as"

- Did the employer treat the individual differently as a result of his or her assumed impairment?

- There are certain predictable assessments that in virtually all cases will indicate protection by the ADAAA

Mental or emotional impairments

- Mental impairments (intellectual disabilities) are a concern to employers

- Employers should have a process in place

- What to do about an inability to get along with others?

"Substantially limits" is not defined by the statute

- What does substantial mean?

- In 2011, the EEOC issued new rules of construction for courts to follow in determining "substantially limits"

- An impairment's impact need not be permanent to be a disability

- Recent EEOC regulations make it clear that disability should be construed broadly

"He or she is otherwise qualified for the position"

- The essential functions of the position are important

- An employer may not terminate or refuse to hire an employee who is "otherwise qualified"

- An employer must determine the essential elements of each position within a firm

- There are some things that an employer cannot consider

- The ADAAA prohibits the use of a test to determine "otherwise qualified" based on uncorrected disability

"Essential functions"

- The Acts require a determination of essential functions

- The term "essential" refers to those tasks which are fundamental

- Employers may not include in their job descriptions incidental responsibilities

Case discussion: Pickens v. Soo Line Railroad Co, *264 F. 3d 773 (8th Cir. 2001)*

"The disability can be reasonably accommodated"

- Reasonable accommodation generally means the removal of unnecessary restrictions or barriers

- Reasonable accommodation does not place an undue burden or hardship on the employer

Undue burden or hardship

- Undue burden or hardship is not limited to financial difficulty

- Some examples of "undue hardship" are not acceptable defenses to a claim of discrimination

Case discussion: Cassidy v. Detroit Edison Company, *138 F. 3d 629 (6th Cir. 1997)*

- The employee should engage in an "interactive process"

"He or she suffered an adverse employment decision"

- Employers have a number of considerations in regard to disability discrimination

- No one yet knows the impact of the ADAAA

- Likely outcomes

- Disability discrimination claims will no longer focus as intently on whether an employee is covered

- Cases will focus on whether the employee and employer properly engaged in the interactive process

- And whether a reasonable accommodation was provided (and if not, why?)

Employers have additional responsibilities in connection with health-related issues

The common law may be involved as well

- An employer's actions may result in a tort claim by the employee

- An employer may owe a common-law tort duty for the protection of co-workers

The Genetic Information Nondiscrimination Act went into effect in 2010

- Title II of GINA applies to employers

- GINA limits employers use of genetic information in three ways

- Prohibits employers from using genetic information to make employment decisions

- Restricts employers from acquiring genetic information about employees and applicants

- Requires employers to keep genetic information confidential

- GINA leaves certain questions unanswered

Conclusion

- Disability discrimination regulation has a long history

- There are requirements to prove the case for disability discrimination

- Employers have a number of considerations in regard to disability discrimination

Retaliation

Introduction

Setting

- Everyone has a natural tendency to strike back

- But it is wrong to strike back for exercising legal rights

- Jurors may be skeptical of discrimination claims ...

- ... but they know retaliation happens

Objective:

- In this lecture, we examine the law of retaliation

A description of retaliation law

Generally, retaliation is an action taken in return for an offense or injury

- Many federal and state statutes relate to retaliation

- Retaliation claims are up

    - 35% over the last decade

    - 43% of all claims

- Recent Supreme Court decisions threaten to open the floodgates further

Retaliation occurs when an employer takes an adverse action against a covered individual because the employee engaged in a protected activity.

- There is no underlying violation required!

- Employers cannot retaliate against those who take advantage of statutorily protected rights

Title VII contains an anti-retaliation provision

- The anti-retaliation provision protects anyone who engages in a "protected activity"

- The anti-retaliation provision prohibits any employer action that "well might have dissuaded a reasonable worker from making or supporting a charge of discrimination."

- Retaliation for the filing of a discrimination claim is discriminatory

- It does not matter if the underlying claim lacks merit

The Supreme Court recently expanded the scope of who can make a retaliation claim

- The Supreme Court broadened the coverage of retaliation claims to include employees who themselves do not engage in "protected activity"

Case discussion: Thompson v. North American Stainless, *131 S.Ct. 863 (2011)*

- The court failed to identify a fixed class of relationships for which third-party reprisals are unlawful

What the employee must prove

Analysis of a retaliation claim follows a similar analytical framework

- Retaliation cases involve the same burden-shifting analysis

- First, the plaintiff makes a prima facie case

- The elements of a prima facie case are

- engagement in a protected activity

- adverse employment action

- causal connection between the two

- The employer may then give a legitimate reason for its action

- The burden shifts back to the employee to show pretext

Retaliation claims fall into two categories

- There are two types of retaliation claims

- Participation claims

- The law protects any form of participation in a proceeding alleging discrimination

- Opposition claims

- Retaliation for opposition to a discriminatory action provides a claim

Proving the retaliation claim

- You must understand the meanings of the following terms:

- Covered Individual

- Protected Activity

- Adverse employment action

- Retaliation claims often rely on circumstantial evidence

What the employer must prove

The employer must establish a legitimate non-discriminatory reason (LNDR)

- How to establish an LNDR defense

- Use plain language

- Be careful when citing to "personality issues"

- Provide a specific reason for termination within a reasonable time

Behavior and culture matter in establishing an LNDR defense

- Fairness matters

- Don't humiliate employees

- Be wary of saying one thing and doing another

- Investigate the complaint and not the complainant

- Put yourself in the employee's shoes

How can an employer minimize retaliation claims?

A three-step strategy

- Create

- Educate

- Investigate

Step one: Create

- Create a retaliation policy that includes

- A definition of retaliation

- A statement that retaliation will not be permitted

- A statement that complaints will be promptly investigated and resolved

- A statement of confidentiality

- The policy should provide specific examples

Step two: Educate

- Educate managers and supervisors on how to prevent retaliation complaints

- The training program should include:

- A description of the company's anti-retaliation policy

- Examples of retaliatory acts or role playing scenarios

- Information on the consequences of illegally retaliating against employees

Step three: Investigate

- Investigate allegations of retaliation and take prompt corrective action when retaliation occurs

- Monitor the treatment of employees who have complained of discrimination

The law may protect an employee where the discharge violates a recognized public policy

Public policy concerns the social, moral, and economic values of a society

- Employers and society may sometimes have competing interests

- What constitutes a violation of public policy?

- Certain acts or contracts are said to be against public policy if they tend to

- promote breach of the law,

- promote breach of the policy behind a law,

- or tend to harm the state or its citizens

Employers may not fire an employee for refusing to commit an illegal act

- Issues may arise when employees engage in conduct that may be socially desirable but not protected by law

- An employee may be protected from discharge for whistleblowing

- The federal whistleblower statute protects certain employees

- A number of states have enacted whistleblowing statutes

- The Sarbanes-Oxley Act provides protection to whistleblowers

Conclusion

- Retaliation is an action taken in return for an offense or injury

- There are means of proving a retaliation claim

- An employer can adopt a strategy to reduce retaliation claims

Restrictions on employee mobility

Introduction

Setting

- The hiring process is difficult

- Employers invest a great deal in finding their employees

- Employers would like to retain employees

- Employees are interested in retaining the freedom to change jobs

Objective

- In this lecture, we examine the means that employers use to retain employees

Most employers will seek to retain employees

Many employers will insist that employees sign some form of noncompete

agreement

- The noncompete has many names

- The noncompete agreement restricts what an employee can do AFTER he leaves his employment

Historically, courts do not like noncompete agreements

- Once, courts refused to enforce noncompete agreements

- A focus on "freedom of contract" changed the manner of dealing with noncompete agreements

- The industrial revolution saw the first routine enforcement of noncompete agreements

- Under this approach, an employer had a right to protect its interests

- Courts recognized the rights of the parties to contract to whatever they wanted to contract to

What is a noncompete agreement?

- A noncompete agreement is an agreement in which an employee agrees to not compete with his employer after employment ends

- The noncompete agreement adds limitations to an employment contract

- Noncompete agreements are generally used in two different situations

- after termination of employment

- in conjunction with the sale of a business

Employers use different forms of contractual agreement to reach the same result

- Noncompete agreements

- Nonsolicitation agreements

- Trade secrets agreements

The common law approach to noncompete agreements is based on reasonableness

Does the noncompete agreement serve a legitimate business purpose?

- The common law seeks to balance interests

  - the interests of the employer

  - the interests of the employee

  - the interests of society

- Traditionally, the courts recognized two primary interests as legitimate justifications for a noncompete agreement

- the employer's interests in protecting the goodwill of the business

- the employer's interests in protecting the trade secrets of the business
- Noncompete agreements are often seen as added protection to a confidentiality agreement

Noncompete agreements often contain four separate yet intermingled clauses

- These clauses are:
- general non-competition
- customer non-solicitation
- employee non-solicitation
- non-disclosure agreements

Enforcement of a noncompete agreement varies from state to state

To be enforceable, the noncompete agreement must be restricted

- Restricted by time
- Restricted by geographic location
- Restricted by scope

Enforcement of a noncompete agreement is a matter of state law

State law differs greatly in its treatment of noncompete agreements

- Some states enforce all reasonable noncompete agreements

- Some states refuse to enforce noncompete agreements

- Some states utilize the 'blue pencil doctrine' to modify agreements

- An argument for abandoning the 'blue pencil' doctrine exists

In recent years, courts in enforcement states have relaxed restrictions

- Courts have broadened the interests that legitimately can be protected by employee noncompete agreements

- Courts have broadened the scope of activities that may be restricted by noncompete agreements

- States have also enacted statutes that make it easier to enforce noncompete agreements

- State courts will often enforce a stepdown provision

Even without a noncompete, a court can sometime enjoin a former employee from working for a competitor

- The "inevitable disclosure" doctrine

Case discussion: IBM v. Johnson, *629 F. Supp. 2d 321 (S.D. New York 2009)*

- The common law duty of loyalty

What are the ramifications of widespread use of the noncompete

agreement?

- Does legal infrastructure determine a region's economy?
- Several studies suggest that the noncompete agreement is actually a drag on a state's economy

Drafting an enforceable noncompete agreement

- Identify the parties and the interest being served
- Create reasonable restrictions on scope, geography, and time
- Include a stepdown agreement if necessary

Conclusion

- Most employers will seek to retain employees by any means necessary

- The common law approach to noncompete agreements is based on reasonableness

- Enforcement of a noncompete agreement varies from state to state

Privacy in employment law

Introduction

Setting

- Employment law involves the balancing of interests

- Courts must balance the interests of employers, employees, and society

- Privacy is a fundamental right

- Courts struggle with balancing privacy interests in the employment context

Objective

- In this lecture, we examine an employee's right to privacy

Where do privacy rights come from?

Privacy rights may derive from multiple sources

- The Constitution protects privacy

- Federal and state statutes protect privacy

- The common law protects privacy

Privacy protections differ based on whether the employee works in the

public or private sector

- Privacy rights in the private sector of employment are limited

- Public sector privacy protections may come from the Constitution

- The Fourth Amendment protects public sector employees

- The Fourth Amendment protects against unreasonable search and seizure

Case discussion: O'Connor v. Ortega, *480 U.S. 709 (1987)*

Why is there a difference between public and private sector employees?

- There are two basic distinctions

- Constitutional rights are not involved because there is no state action

- Government employees need more protection because of the amount of power the government holds

What rights does a private sector employee have?

- Private sector employees may rely on statutory law or the common law

- Some state legislatures have provided statutory protection

- Most private sector employees must depend on the common law to protect privacy rights

The common law provides a right to collect damages for invasion of privacy

Intrusion into seclusion

- Elements of an intrusion into seclusion claim

- the defendant employer intentionally intruded into a private area

- the plaintiff was entitled to privacy in that area, and

- the intrusion would be objectionable to a person of reasonable sensitivity.

Case discussion: Smyth v. The Pillsbury Company, *914 F. Supp 97 (N.D. Penn. 1996)*

Public disclosure of private facts

- Elements of a public disclosure of private facts claim

- there was an intentional or negligent public disclosure

- of private matters, and

- such disclosure would be objectionable to a reasonable person of ordinary sensitivities.

Case discussion: Yoder v. Ingersoll-Rand Company, *31 F. Supp. 2d 565 (N.D. Ohio 1997)*

Defamation

- Elements of a defamation claim

    - false and defamatory words concerning employee

    - negligently or intentionally communicated to a third party without the employee's consent (publication)

    - resulting harm to the employee defamed

- There are defenses to a defamation claim

Publication in a false light

- Elements of publication in a false light

    - there was a public disclosure

    - of facts that place the employee in a false light before the public

    - if the false light would be highly offensive to a reasonable person, and

- if the person providing the information had knowledge of or recklessly disregarded the falsity or false light of the publication.

Case discussion: Peoples Bank & Trust Co. v. Globe Int'l, Inc., *786 F. Supp. 791 (D. Ark. 1992)*

- A false light claim resembles defamation

- Defamation must harm one's reputation; the false light tort does not

What are my employees doing? How can I find out?

Specific issues of employee privacy

- Telephone and voice mail

- Computer monitoring

- Bugging employee conversations

- Mail interception

There are privacy issues with physical searches

- Locker searches

- Office/desk searches

- Car searches

There may be privacy implications in testing

- Polygraph examinations

- Psychological and integrity testing

- Drug testing

There may be privacy implications in surveillance

Case discussion: French v. United Parcel Service, Inc., *2 F. Supp. 2d 128 (D.C. Mass. 1998)*

- Regulating off-duty conduct is risky

- Does the off-duty conduct impact the workplace?

Conclusion

- Privacy is a fundamental right in the United States

- Differences exist in the treatment of public and private sector employees

- An employer must take caution in monitoring employees

Social media and employment law

Introduction

Setting

- Social media has become part of daily life

- Social media presents unique problems for employers

- Employers are struggling with the proper response

- Employers need to develop a social media strategy

Objective

- In this lecture, we look at potential problems and proposed employer strategies

Social media is problematic

Social media is about interaction

- Social media has killed our private lives

- Our evolving notion of what is "private" has broad legal effects

- Humans are social animals

Social media use has exploded

- Technology has made communication to large numbers of people instantaneously

- Almost every employee carries a computer and a camera in their pocket

- Communication may occur without the employee's direct involvement

The use and risks of social media

- Social media use changes faster than we are able to forecast the risk

- Risk begins with individual employees but may expose employers

- Organizations may reduce risk for both individuals and the organization

- But expect the risks to evolve as well

There are three potential problems with employees' use of social media

- Disclosure of things they should not disclose

- Harming a third person with their communication

- Violating the law (intentionally or unintentionally)

There are potential employment related legal issues in conjunction with social media

An employer may be liable for hostile work environment enforcement

Case discussion: Blakey v. Continental Airlines, Inc., *751 A.2d 538 (N.J. 2000)*

- Potential employer liability is based on knowledge

- An employer may be charged with knowledge (constructive knowledge)

Case discussion: Wolfe v. Fayetteville Sch. Dist*, 600 F. Supp. 2d 1011 (W.D. Ark. 2009*

- Employers may have a duty to monitor social media

- An employee may overcome the employer's defense by showing pretext

- Inconsistent assessment

- Inconsistent enforcement

An employer may be liable for a defamation claim

- Claims of defamation often arise out of online activity

Case discussion: Collins v. Purdue University et al., *703 F. Supp. 2d 862 (N.D. Ind. 2010)*

Case discussion: In re Perry, *423 B.R. 215 (Bkrtcy. S.D. Tex. 2010)*

- A policy may help

- a policy that makes it clear that online statements by managers do not represent the views of the employer and

- are not part of the manager's duties should assist in arguing that the statement was not made in the course and scope of employment.

An employer may be liable for invasion of privacy

- The online disclosure of truthful but sensitive personal information may support an invasion of privacy claim

Case discussion: Yath v. Fairview Clinics, N.P., *767 N.W.2d 34 (Minn. App. 2009)*

An employer may be liable for the violation of a statute

- HIPAA

- Securities regulations

- Copyright and trademark issues

What happens if you fire an employee based on social media issues?

The National Labor Relations Act may protect the terminated employee

- Employees may engage in protected discussions regarding the terms and conditions of employment.

Case discussion: Quigley v. Giblin, *569 F. 3d 449 (D.C. Cir. 2009)*

The common law may protect the terminated employee

- An employer may also face an invasion of privacy claim based on the employer's review of an employee's electronic activity.

Case discussion: Quon v. City of Ontario, et al, *529 F. 3d 892 (9th Cir. 2009).*

Title VII may protect the terminated employee

- Discipline against an employee based on membership in protected classes is illegal

- Employers should be careful of religious claims

A flexible social media policy can be beneficial

How can an employer protect itself?

- An employer may be liable for its employee's acts

- Under certain circumstances, an employer may be limited in its ability to discipline its employees for social media use

- An employer should develop social media strategies

Keep federal and state law in mind

- Be mindful of the provisions of the National Labor Relations Act

- Some states have limiting an employer's ability to terminate an employee based on lawful activity

- conducted outside of working hours and

- away from the employer's premises

Drafting a social media policy

- Encourage respectful use of social media by all employees

- Address different expectations for work hours and non-work hours

- Address use of company resources and time

- Eliminate or reduce expectation of privacy

- Reinforce nature of confidentiality obligations

- Address manager use issues

- Provide a complaint system

- Outline potential discipline

Conclusion

- Social media is problematic

- There are potential employment related legal issues

- A flexible social media policy can be beneficial

About the author

Griffin Pivateau is the Puterbaugh Professor of Ethics and Legal Studies in Business at the Spears School of Business at Oklahoma State University, specializing in employment law. His research interests focus on the intersection between law and business strategy, assisting business managers to achieve competitive advantage using the law. He has written extensively on matters of employee mobility and retention. His research has been cited by numerous courts and other scholars.

Before joining the faculty at Oklahoma State University, Pivateau practiced law in New Orleans, Louisiana and Houston, Texas. Pivateau graduated from the University of Texas School of Law. Prior to law school, he attended graduate school at Southern Methodist University, where he studied Spanish Colonial America under the direction of well-known scholar David J. Weber.